Agile

Essentials of Team and Project Management.

Manifesto for Agile Software Development

Book Description

Leading an Agile team calls for unexpected changes and typical project management tactics. You simply can't approach an Agile Project with the same mentality as you usually use. Agile teams are self-organized, self-directing, and lack a hierarchical structure that often defines project management. But even with the lack of common elements, you can be a team leader and guide your project to success. Even if you're not familiar with coding or software development, understanding the Agile manifesto, and the basics of Agile project management, you can be a valued part of the team.
Within this book you'll learn:

- The principles of Agile development
- Different methods to guide your team toward success
- How to keep team members accountable
- Your role within the Agile team and how to best act as a leader
- How to address conflict and tension within your team
- Valuable tools to use to help your team communicate clearly and collaborate effectively
- How to manage the events that drive Agile projects

Managing an Agile project can go smoothly if you use the principles and constructs of an Agile team the way they were intended. Some modern tools have made that even easier, but you'll always need to have a grip on the human element of team management as well. By expanding your knowledge of Agile, you can balance the importance of people, the usefulness of tools, and the value of the principles laid out in the Agile Manifesto.

Table of Contents

Introduction

Leading a new team of people with different personalities, experiences, and backgrounds can seem like a difficult task. Fortunately, the principles that guide Agile Projects and project management create a team environment that should foster productivity and collaborative thinking. With the right tools in place, a focus on collective processes, and a system for handling any obstacles or stumbling block, you can see your Agile Project through to completion. Support your team with the foundation of the Agile Manifesto, create your own team manifesto or guidelines for a particular project, and learn how to lead a group of unique individuals toward a common goal.

If this is your first large project to manage, you'll have the opportunity to explore which Agile systems fit your leadership style and team. If you are an ace with project management but new to the team or to Agile Principles, this book will help you explore the systematic approach necessary to develop Agile software.

Chapter 1: Understanding Agile and Agile Manifesto

Agile describes an approach to project development and specific projects relating to software development. This approach allows developers and coders to work with greater autonomy and an improved focus on quality rather than fulfilling a certain function on a team. In short, this iterative approach to development uses increments to ensure quality results.

In 2001, a group of top developers came together and created the Manifesto for Agile Software Development. The group of men who brought these ideas and principles together had led their field in development by drastically changing team dynamics and the approach to project management. The Agile founders were those who developed and represented Extreme Programming or XP, Adaptive Software, Crystal, Pragmatic Programming, DSDM, and SCRUM. Although they had structural differences, these systems for development all broke down to the need to emphasize the value of the developers and team members rather than focusing on getting the product completed. Together they moved to take power away from corporate executives and managers who were unfamiliar with the software development processes and demands.

That goal of redirecting the power dynamic and the abilities to manage or control a team led to a substantial amount of strife across many industries. Virtually anyone who needed software developed was told that they needed to follow Agile principles and methodology, and that would mean they would have no control over the team or project.

It is important to emphasize that the lack of control or absence of a hierarchical structure does not mean that there isn't a purpose for managing the project. Team members, SCRUM masters, and champions have key positions and roles to play. There are still deadlines, attainable goals, and specific steps necessary to see the project to completion.

What is Agile – And What Agile is Not

One of the most common misconceptions is that Agile Development is a methodology or an approach to software development. Agile is a set of principles accompanied by values that, in theory, should advance idea generation and implementation within the creative process. There are multiple goals of Agile Software Development, and there are different methodologies for approaching an Agile Project.

While chapter two will layout the principles in full, we will quickly overview the core values so you can get acquainted with what exactly Agile promotes. The core values came into place because when the Agile Manifesto came together, these were particular struggles that software developers and coders experienced. These are still common challenges within an Agile Project. But the core values in the Agile Manifesto have turned the tables, and now these core values can make it more difficult for project managers and champions.

The core values of Agile include placing individuals or the people involved in development over the processes and tools used to complete a project. Well, it seems that this value should go without saying, if you look at nearly any department within a business, you'll see that the tools in the processes are valued much more highly than the people involved. When it comes to software development and a project which could easily go awry with the incorrect placement of a semi-colon, it is important that you listen to your team.

Make sure that you value your team and make sure that they know they're valued. Project leaders and managers will often appreciate their teams, but the teams won't feel that firsthand and they can easily become disgruntled.

Additionally, Agile Developers value working software over excessive documentation or documentation that the people outside of the coding team can understand. Before Agile executives and high-level managers would put excessive documentation demands on coding teams. Then they would be quite upset when they would read the documentation and not understand it. Essentially the only people who need to understand documentation relevant to software development are the people working on the software for either building it or updating it later. If you can't understand the documentation that your team provides, feel free to ask questions. But you should hesitate to demand that they change their documentation practices as they may be using a uniform method.

Agile teams also put a high value on collaboration between the customer and the team. For Agile teams, one of the customers is the business itself. This intense focus on value often takes over contract negotiation in that an Agile Contract may read more as a general guideline than a list of expectations.

Finally, Agile teams demand the ability to respond to change quickly and giving priority to change over following a strict plan. This is a particular challenge for project managers. You may have a plan all laid out with milestones, and within just a few days, that entire plan can be thrown out. You will need to develop soft skills such as adaptability, compromise abilities, and creative problem-solving. This doesn't mean that the Agile Team tells you what happens. What this means is that you need to come together with your team and collaborate to determine a new plan that accommodates the changes as well.

Just to summarize, Agile is not a methodology or approach to project management. Agile is a collection of values and principles that should guide a software Development Team toward the successful development of software. As you learn more about Agile and the systems of project management that fit into Agile Software Development, you'll see why software development requires a different approach in order to succeed.

Goals of Agile

So what are the goals of Agile? The Agile Manifesto and the leaders of software development in that time came together with specific goals in mind. The primary goal which should benefit any business was to satisfy the customers. When it comes to Agile Projects, the customer is both the business and the end-user. That means that the developers are not only looking out for what is effective and efficient for the business to support but also meaningful to the people who will use the software daily.

They placed the goal of satisfying customers above all other goals and believed that the four core values of Agile Software Development feed into this singular goal.

The second goal of Agile is to create a project which inspires the contributors. The meaning here is that software development should always be an exciting process because resources and demands change constantly. It is one of the few fields that allows work in the form of projects that demands constant creative problem-solving. The people contributing should always bring something to the table, and with Agile, if you're simply showing up for your job, then you're not an inspiring contributor.

The remaining goals of Agile borrow from some of the very specific principles from the Agile Manifesto in order to guide these projects.

For example, one is that interaction should be done in person. This reflects other specific principles from the Agile Manifesto, but the underlying goal here is to ensure that all communication is clear and concise.

Defining the Goals of Your Project

When you're defining the goals of your project, consider the goals of Agile Software Development. Various sections of this book will revisit how to define, set, and uphold goals for your Agile Project. However, there is some foundational information to help you move forward with understanding exactly how to define a goal in conjunction with Agile Goals, principles, and values.

When working on an Agile Project, goals should express a directive, and improve morale among team members.

That's a lot to expect from a list of goals. However, when writing your goals, you'll want to assess its extrinsic and intrinsic value to the team. For example, if you have a goal such as "Create thorough and comprehensive documentation daily," that goal might drag down the morale of the team. However, a goal such as "Collectively create thorough and comprehensive documentation" could help pull the team together.

Keep these thoughts and suggestions in mind whenever you start to map out Agile Goals:

- Keep your goal simple and concise enough to fit on a sticky note.

- Ensure that there is only one interpretation of the goal.

- Not every goal has to be actionable, but every goal must serve a purpose.

- Will the team commit to the goal?

- Does the goal excite or ignite?

The reason for addressing goal-setting so early into this book is to establish that setting goals for Agile Teams are very different from creating goals for other projects. Many project managers create goals straight from their task list. With Agile Teams, the task list or Kanban board will guide the team members, but again, because of the drastic daily changes, these tasks may change as well. It is easier to approach goal setting for Agile Teams with a broader or more overarching purpose.

Overview of Methodologies

The many different demands of developing work calls for a different approach to handling the project management elements. As you read through this book, you'll learn about the basic elements and principles of the Agile Method and how you can use these principles to guide your team through your project.

The common challenge among Agile Project Leaders is that the different methodologies may apply to a project in different ways. There may be times that a methodology doesn't come into play at all during a project. Then there are other times where you may use a wide variety of the methodologies in varying capacities for a single project. You will surely learn more about the principles which govern Agile Software Development. However, you'll need to use your leadership and communication skills to determine which methodology is applied to your project and which fit your team.

Agile Methodologies include, but are not limited to :

- **Scrum** – Lightweight framework that demands small increments of work driven based on productivity and simplicity.

- **Lean** – Use value stream mapping to deliver high value to the customer (end-user) and is highly flexible.

- **Extreme Programming or XP** – The focus is on speed and continuous delivery, usually used to continue software improvement.

- **Crystal** – Often called the most flexible Agile Method, it focuses on communication and team reflection to identify what did or did not work.

- **DSDM** – A method that focuses on delivering the "useful 80% part of the system in 20% of the time."

- **Feature Driven Development** – Uses a model list with features to drive the iterations and development process.

- **Kanban** – Visual method for working and is often used alongside other methodologies. Project management through tracking works in progress and future tasks.

Again, when developing an Agile Project, you are not limited to a single methodology. Using grab portions from different Agile Methodologies and use them together. Alternatively, you may use a single methodology. How and what you use is determined by you and the Agile team. As the project manager, you're likely the champion for the company and the project meaning that you are the bridge between the Agile Team and the desired result. With proper project management and Agile Techniques, you can help your team develop highly functional software through proven techniques and systems.

Chapter 2: Implementing Agile Principles

The Agile Manifesto came together in Snowbird, Utah. It certainly wasn't a tech innovation hub or the unlikely town of eager entrepreneurs. It was a vacation town where the leaders of Lightweight - what would eventually become known as Agile - software development came together in 2001 to write the Agile Manifesto. The Manifesto itself reads as a type of Declaration of Independence. The Manifesto itself has a short opening about the intent of software developers around the world, four core values, and the signatures of the leaders who came together. However, the Manifesto is not complete without the 12 principles of Agile Software Development. These twelve principles were put together at the same meeting and have guided software development since 2001.

The principles and values feed into one another and lend themselves towards creating a productive and successful team. However, it's up to the team and project manager/champion to understand how to implement these principles. Within chapter two, you will get the opportunity to dive into each principle and learn how to implement it within an Agile Team.

Principle One: Highest Priority is to Satisfy the Customer through Early and Continuous Delivery of Valuable Software

One of the most commonly misunderstood principles is the very first one. The first principle of Agile Software Development is to place the highest priority on customer satisfaction

And to execute that priority early and through ongoing software delivery. Unlike other teams such as research and development, or manufacturing teams, it is possible to deliver software in chunks.

Agile teams will often deliver software in functional segments. That means that as soon as the software is functioning, it goes through a release. Then when an additional function or feature is available, it undergoes another release. This continues for the life of the product. Even when all features are available and working to the best of the developer's ability, the product will need updates and patches.

For project managers and the team, this can become an overwhelming task to take on. It is very easy for teams to become disheartened, knowing that there isn't a finish line or an end date for this project. However, it also allows the team to better focus on quality and value because they aren't rushing to meet one deadline that determines success or failure.

Application within the Team

This first principle is what largely allows Agile teams to be self-organizing. What the champion or project manager should go through with the team is the expectations, functions, and current demands of the software. It is largely up to the team to determine when segments will be available for release, which is most important to work on first, and how they will arrange for software delivery.

Between the team and the project manager or the champion, there will be constant face-to-face communication specifically relating to releases and the delivery of the software. These are sometimes called standups or Kanban meetings.

Impact on Team and Project Managers

Leaders are put into an uncomfortable position with principle one because they have to learn to accept that they will receive many small pieces that will eventually make a completed system. You will need to work to understand that a single release may only address a particular task or one function within the software.

To accommodate this, you'll need to ensure that face-to-face communication is both consistent and easy. It was mentioned earlier that there are daily meetings such as stand up meetings, but there are other forms of communication that can help the project managers or the team managers understand the flow of development and progress.

Everything relating to principle one is about communication and strategy. In addition to the ongoing communication efforts, you'll need to create a big picture strategy that closely looks at the problems the software needs to address. Additionally, you'll need to dive into the expected outcomes. Work with your team closely to identify the core functions of the project. Again the plan should be brief and simple to align with Agile core values. It is a lot to ask. But to summarize:

To best satisfy the customer and provide early and continuous delivery of valuable software, the team and champions must work together to have a plan and strategy which addresses the customer's needs and the team's expected outcomes.

Principle Two: Welcome Changing Requirements, Even Late in Development.

Agile Processes Harness Change for the Customer's Competitive Advantage

Principle two is a little more straightforward than principle one because it largely has to do with change. This is one of the few principles that lends itself more to the customers, i.e., the business and the end-user, than the team itself. Agile teams must accept changed requirements even very late into the development stages. Again for many team members, this can lower morale and seem as though the project will never be done. It is part of the champion or project managers roll to ensure that even when changes come late into the game, the focus stays on creating a valuable product rather than closing out the project.

Often when people reference this principle, they are looking at the secondary portion, the segment of the principle which reads that the team should grab hold of changes to give the customer a competitive advantage. Within Agile, one of the customers is the business, and if you can give the business a competitive advantage, then it is more likely that more people will use the software.

Often when you come across software that users simply hate, it's because the team was unwilling to make changes or adapt to accommodate the end-user. Those problems can be avoided when the team understands that giving the business a competitive advantage is also an advantage for the software.

Application within the Team

Agile teams must have a well-developed sense of change acceptance. Prior to Agile, the only philosophy guiding software development was the waterfall method, which explicitly resisted change. But in order to adapt to change easily and to make accepting change less of a struggle, Agile Teams need to avoid getting stuck in red tape.
The change should also be able to come from the team. The team should feel confident enough to approach managers with ideas that could produce a higher value product.

Impact on Team and Project Management

Management and champions can have a substantial impact on how the team feels about change. Approach the team when you understand that a change is necessary for the business to have a competitive advantage or for the software to avoid being outdated by the time it gets released. However, don't approach the team with every possible change that the business might consider.

Managers or champions should be dedicated to a change before approaching the team. They should also take into consideration the team's input and insight regarding that specific change.

Principle Three: Deliver Working Software Frequently with Preference to a Shorter Timescale

The third Agile principle really only relates to frequent or consistent delivery. This is where Agile Teams need to define delivery, working software, and frequently means to them.

Work with your team because it is possible that your team could produce weekly deliveries, whereas other teams may need months to make a delivery.

Principle Four: Businesspeople and Developers Must Work Together Daily through the Project

Communication is such an integral part of Agile Teams. The primary goal of this principle is to establish that the coding team and the business people involved in the project can't be wildly divided. The team must interact with stakeholders, stakeholders must interact with champions, and champions and stakeholders must interact with the team.

While each person is responsible for their contribution to open communication, they are also responsible for keeping other people involved in the communication process.

Application within the Team

The team will have many meetings and should work within close proximity to each other so that whenever discussions are had, all the team members are privy to the information.
Additionally, the team will need to participate in daily standups or Kanban meetings. The team will also need to meet with all the businesspersons involved during reflecting meetings.

Impact on Team and Project Management

You may need to adopt the most flexible and understanding open door policy you've ever experienced in your professional career. You may also need to move your desk or physically work nearer the coding team to ensure that they have access to one of the businesspersons involved in the project at all times. If you're the Scrum Master or the leader of the coding team, then you'll need to ensure that you have a direct line of communication with the champion or stakeholders involved in the project.

Principle Five: Build Projects through Motivated Individuals
Give Them the Environment and Support Needed.

Trust Them to Get the Job Done.

This is the principle where the Agile Team really puts their needs back on the project or team manager. It is going to be your responsibility not just to motivate the team but trusting them. That means you may need to drop micromanaging habits and questions such as, "Are you sure?"

The team will need an environment and a lot of support from all of the leaders involved either on the business end or on the coding end. It also means that the company needs to be understanding about the degree of challenge involved in software development. "Riding" an employee, especially a coder, will only result in frustration and a much lower quality product.

Principle Six: Face-to-Face Conversation is the Most Efficient and Effective Method of Conveying Information

Principle six is a particular problem for modern Agile Teams. Even back in 2001, teams were more likely to fall back on email and memos, which are ineffective for communication and conveying information. Now with project management systems such as Asana, Trello, Monday, and chat features in almost every project management tool, it is even more difficult to promote face-to-face conversation.

Application within the Team

 The most common way that Agile Teams ensure they communicate face to face more than through alternative communication is to sit in close proximity. Take down the cubicle dummy walls and allow your team to sit in a collective desk. Or allow them to have their spaces but keep the air in the room open. Don't put up walls, don't separate the team.

The purpose of keeping your team in an open space and working in such close proximity is convenience. You want to make it more convenient to turn in your chair and say something to a team member than it is to type a quick chat or text.

Impact on Team and Project Management

Throughout this book, you'll see the mention of stand-up meetings, Kanban meetings, and reflection meetings. These are critical, and some of these meetings will need to happen daily. If team and project managers don't take the time in their schedule for these meetings, then they may be the primary problem in any issue or challenge that the project experiences. Principle Seven: Working Software is the Primary Measure of Progress

It should go without saying that working software is the measure of progress, but it doesn't. In fact, principle seven is often overlooked and has led to some of the biggest technological disappointments and failures within recent history. Common examples of teams that have ignored

principle 7 include the initial iTunes to Windows Operating System release and Windows ME.

Windows ME is a typical favorite for people exploring this principle because, by and large, it didn't work. Copying a file from one location to another could take minutes or hours.That's not diving into the bugs and glitches that plagued the system.

Application within the Team

This is one area where teams must stand up to process owners, champions, and businesspersons involved in the project. If the software doesn't work, then it's not ready for release. However, teams may suggest released beta versions, knowing that there are bugs or glitches, in an effort to rely on user activity to reveal root problems.

Impact on Team and Project Management

Managers must be very careful not to push a team to release a product that will only result in disappointment or frustration. If a software doesn't work correctly, it may be as simple as an extra space or inverted number sequence. But the act of going through the coding to identify and then correct the area is not so simple. Teams need time, and trust, from their managers to ensure that software works properly.

Additionally, managers should give some consideration to the functionality of the software as progress. From day to day, a feature or segment of the software becoming more functional is an outstanding sign of success.

Principle Eight: Agile Processes Promote Sustainable Development.

The Sponsors, Developers and Users Should be Able to Maintain a Constant Pace Indefinitely

An Agile project certainly isn't a marathon, but instead is a series of sprints. The term "sprints" applies to the iterations or the short runs that the team works within. However, sprints don't inherently set a constant pace. It's left to the project leaders to establish the pace, and it is up to the team to maintain that pace indefinitely. Everyone involved must be able to work at the same pace, which can be extremely difficult to manage.

Application within the Team

When something seems to be taking too long, give the team the reins. Allow the team to conduct a root cause analysis to identify where you're working harder rather than working smarter. Your team should have enough trust from leadership to evaluate productivity and challenge the status quo.

But, your team might be facing a natural ebb and flow when it comes to changes in pace. Give your team access to all the resources necessary to execute with peak performance during peak hours or seasons for your business. Then, ensure that they put their effort into pushing forward during the slower times as well. Even though it seems that coding teams are largely segmented from the rest of the business, they feel the same intensity and lulls as everyone else.

Impact on Team and Project Management
Having your team work longer or harder isn't the answer. A pace must be sustainable, maintainable,

and natural. While you may certainly need to intervene and address times when there are distractions, most of the time, you should allow the team to control pacing.

Your role in team or project management when working with an Agile Team will likely include removing unnecessary processes and obstacles. For example, if a manager wants to approve all changes in the development plan as they arise, your role might be to convince them that it would hurt the team and severely impact the project in a negative way. However, you might also compromise and invite them into some of the sit-down meetings to see the changes in the plan firsthand.

Principle Nine: Continuous Attention to Technical Excellence and Good Design Enhances Agility

For many people, principle 9 is the core of confusion with Agile Development Techniques. After all, the remaining 11 principles refer to guidelines to get software out quickly as long as it's working. In fact, the general belief around Agile is that it's the quick and dirty software development method. However, this principle is the one that brings the teams involved back to quality, because doing software development with the "quick and dirty" approach simply doesn't work.

Application within the Team

Agile teams largely focus on automating anything that can be automated and closely monitoring everything else. In fact, if there is anything "low-quality" with a project, the team will likely identify the lack of quality first. This is where trust comes into play. If your team says that something needs improvement, go with it.

Impact on Team and Project Management

Even the best of Agile Teams need help working in the right direction and challenging the status quo. Within a management capacity, you can ask when there are better alternatives available, and when you can explore additional technology to provide more valuable results.

The best place to start with this principle is to by getting proven frameworks into place and building a team of individuals who value high-quality work.

Principle Ten: Simplicity – the Art of Maximizing the Amount of Work Not Done Is Essential

Linus Torvalds, the creator of Linux, the open-source operating system, once delivered this prolific statement. He said, "Avoiding complexity reduces bugs. " He is right, and the Agile Leaders who wrote the Manifesto already understood this concept. When you build a project around simplicity, you largely reduce the likelihood of error.

Application within the Team

Simplicity isn't the only aspect of this principle. In fact, the larger portion of the principle is a focus on maximizing the work that is not done. The team may need to extensively discuss this when it comes to determining which processes or steps to skips. What's worse is that leadership will often see this as cutting corners, but ultimately it can produce a high-quality product.

With every team, there is a learning process. The team members must collectively assess and identify what is and is not necessary for the project. Additionally, some members may champion or campaign for certain elements, or features that aren't necessary and simplifying the project,

And not including those features could cause tension within the team. This rule demands that everyone keep their focus on the quality of the product, not simply what they desire as part of the outcome.

Impact on Team and Project Management

Automation, systems, and habit will help to engage this principle within your team. Whenever you have to question why something is taking so long, or why there is a multitude of errors, don't ask what went wrong, or why things are going slow. Ask the team these questions:

- Is there something we can automate?

- Is a lack of systematic handling leading to inconsistencies, bugs, and other problems?

- Do we need to make 'x' a habit?

Asking these questions will help you cultivate trust, and keep the team largely self-lead. It gives them the opportunity to take charge of any problems when simplicity is clearly the answer. However, leaders should also watch their behavior to ensure they're not adding in unnecessary rules or steps that could overcomplicate a project.

Principle Eleven: The Best Architectures, Requirements and Designs Emerge from Self-Organizing Teams

By design, self-organizing teams can easily overtake alternative teams in both productivity and quality of output. When teams are allowed to self-organize and propel themselves toward success, they can take greater ownership over the product and generally manage their responsibility with greater prowess.

Managers need to understand that it is important to take a step back without becoming uninvolved. Allow teams to distribute work, to collaborate, and exchange ideas.

Principle Twelve: At Regular Intervals, the Team Reflects on How to Become More Effective, Then Tunes and Adjusts Behavior Accordingly

This final principle sets the stage for the remainder of this book. Reflection is one of the critical elements in regularly meeting, adjusting, and fine-tuning. The team and leadership will all experiment, test, and then reflect. There are many times when a change caused more work than necessary or that a revised version of the software was found to be less functional than the prior version.

The process of meeting, reflecting, changing, and adjusting is an ongoing circle in nearly every methodology within the Agile umbrella. Retrospectives or Sprint Retrospective meetings will determine what steps the team takes next, and how changes impact the team and the project. However, retrospectives are only part of the reflection process. The lessons learned from one retrospective will come up and help direct the team during the next sprint planning meeting, the sprint review, and may even affect the team during daily standups.

For managers and leaders, retrospection, and discussions about becoming more effective can be a challenge. After all, you're supposed to create a productive and encouraging environment. So, how can you deliver critique and reflection on what was ineffective or inefficient? These meetings are put into place so that everyone can be involved in the discussion,

And because the team is self-organized, if you offer some critique that doesn't align with the rest of the group, it may be seen as unfounded.

In chapter three, you'll learn more about the roles in an Agile Team and how team or project management roles impact Agile Projects.

Chapter 3: Scrum Team Management and Conflict Resolution

Although Scrum certainly isn't used in every Agile Project, the Scrum team framework is almost always present. A Scrum team allows the project to contain only three primary roles, which ensures that there is no unintentional hierarchical structure. However, even with only three primary functions, there will be conflict, the attempt at a hierarchical structure, and challenges within the team in terms of cooperation.

By understanding the roles and learning how to help resolve conflict, you can engage every member of the team. When you're using a well-established framework such as Agile, you're going to have conflict, and people who don't quite fit the mold or don't want to adhere to the principles and values. It happens. But while you're working a project, you need to get buy-in and get everyone on board with their position or role.

Product Owner

The Product Owner is the executive stakeholder. Sometimes they are called 'the Champion' while other times they're referred to as the project manager, project owner, process owner, captain, or many other names. Essentially, they have the final word, and if you're reading this with the intent of leading a project, it is likely that you're either the Product Owner or the Scrum Master (more on that in a moment).

What does the Product Owner do? They're the only established person "in charge" in a hierarchical manner. The original definition through the Scrum guidebook is :

"... is responsible for maximizing the value of the product resulting from the work of the Development Team."

However, the guidebook also states that the Scrum Team will largely help determine how much involvement the Product Owner has. Every project will call for different levels of involvement, engagement, and coaching. It is important to note that the Product Owner is mostly responsible for the outcome of the project. The Product Owner is the only person that is responsible for managing the Backlog. It is possible, and even reasonable that the Development Team will create the Backlog, but again, the Product Owner is responsible for it. SCRUM claims that there's a necessary Product Owner Certification, but many businesses rely on the information publicly available about Scrum and Agile to develop an internal Product Owner. Additionally, because Agile is equivalent to "open-source" in terms of information availability, it is possible to access most of the information from the original Agile Leaders on this role without going through a formal training structure.

The Product Owner's full scope of responsibilities can include:

- Creating the Backlog of "to-do" items

- Reviewing deliverables before arranging for product delivery

- Address or request changes

- Have the deepest understanding of the end user's needs

When you're looking at the wide variety of situations and responsibilities, everything comes back to one sentiment: the Product Owner is responsible for helping the team to create the most valuable product possible. During that process, they should help better the team and lead them through all challenges the team faced while working on the project.

For many people, the Product Owner is the person that's seen as the manager. If someone from outside of the Agile Team were to approach someone with a request or concern, it's likely that they would approach the Product Owner. However, the Product Owner doesn't have any real hierarchical power over the Development Team or the Scrum Master. In fact, if there is any construct of power within the team, it is based purely on respect and can be lost quickly. Recall that Agile teams work because they are self-organized and mostly self-leading.

New Product Owners will often make the mistake of working as though this is a standard project. They act as a manager rather than a facilitator or a guide. However, the Product Owners aren't the only ones who need to adapt their management mentality.

Scrum Master

One of the key differences between Agile Teams and nearly all other teams is that the perceived manager or leader is not the person upholding accountability. The Scrum Master, an elected member of the Development Team who takes on a "player-coach" role, is the one keeping people accountable.

In the line of ensuring that a hierarchical structure is not in place, the Scrum Master, who will lead meetings and hold people responsible, is also a member of the Development Team. They must be a trusted manager who has worked with successful teams in the past and who is comfortable measuring progress under Agile Definitions. A Scrum Master doesn't have to be an experienced Agile Manager, although they should be familiar with the Agile Workflow and positions.

A Scrum Master will take on the following duties:

- Update the Scrum/Kanban board daily

- Follow up on task levels and completions.

- Conduct analyses to determine efficiency and productivity

- Calls together the daily standup meetings

- Determines how to reduce friction within the workflow

- Commands accountability from both the Development Team and the Product Owner.

Although you would think it would fall to the Product Owner, it is usually the Scrum Master's job to ensure that everyone is completing their tasks, getting the help they need, and working with the team's agreed-upon processes. They are also the primary bridge for communication between the Product Owner and the Development Team.

For example, if a member of the Development Team does not thoroughly understand the expectations of the Product Owner for a particular function, it would fall to the Scrum Master to gain clarification. Initially, this seems like a chain of command. That very hierarchical structure that Agile claims don't exist within its many methodologies, including Scrum. However, the use of the Scrum Master as a bridge for communication is not hierarchical. The Development Team can and occasionally will approach the Product Owner with questions and concerns.

The use of the Scrum Master, however, provides a higher level of communication skills. Developers and coders often fall into using jargon and abbreviations that anyone outside of coding or developing wouldn't understand. The Scrum Master takes that jargon and those commonly-used abbreviations among Development Teams and translates them into a common language that the Product Owner, who is usually a businessperson, can easily understand.

Becoming a Scrum Master doesn't come from an assignment to the position. The Product Owner is not responsible for choosing the Scrum Master. The Development Team will choose their Scrum Master and provide an offer. However, the Product Owner can give their input. For example, if the Development Team chooses the most senior member of their team as the Scrum Master, the Product Owner might call to attention that they are simply enlisting the person with the most experience, not necessarily the person with the best communication skills. If you were approached to be a Scrum Master and you accepted the offer, then you should be very proud that your team thinks so highly of you and that the Product Owner likely has a high degree of respect for you as well.

Development Team

The Development Team can have a number of people and most Agile Development Teams average between two and five team members, not including the Scrum Master or the Product Owner. These team members make up the greater majority of the Agile Team, and often their only focus is on software development. That means that even if these team members are part of your long-term IT department, their focus during software development should be exclusive to the Agile Project. These team members stand apart from other developers or coders who may be able because they are specialists in accepting assignments, working collaboratively, and essentially getting the job done.

The Development Team is often formed by the Product Owner and collaboration with the team member's immediate managers if they are concurrent employees. Being approached to be part of an Agile Development Team can be a pretty special point in your career because you're being acknowledged for your ability to work independently and work well within a team. Additionally, Development Team members are often recognized for their creative thinking abilities. That is often how Development Teams will choose the Scrum Master. They'll look for the person who is most capable of communicating clearly and working to solve problems and resolve conflict creatively.

Team members will often work closely with each other, and they'll review each other's code and look at different ways to make all of their work easier and faster. There is no one set task list that applies to all Development Teams the way that the Product Owner, in Scrum Master, had a generalized responsibilities list. The Development Team will do whatever they need to in order to progress with the project. Of course, progress is defined as functioning software.

Finally, it's important to note for Scrum Masters and Product Owners that not every member of the Development Team needs to have a history of working on an Agile Team. Often Agile projects will include a handful of people that have never worked with Agile Development before. In regard to that, the Development Team will often take charge of the greater majority of the project, but they will still require direction. Even those experienced in working on Agile Projects will need support and guidance.

Addressing Complaints

There's not a single or project or a team in existence that hasn't experienced some type of complaint.

However, Agile Complaints tend to be repetitive. From project to project and from team to team, most Agile Projects lead to the same or similar complaints.

The most common Agile complaints include:

- "The organizational culture doesn't fit Agile Values."

o The purpose of Agile values and the Manifesto is that they exist because companies frequently, if not always, don't have a culture that fits with Agile values.

- "There's a resistance to change within the organization."

o Development Teams should only worry about the development, and let the Product Owner handle the struggle with change resistance within the organization.

- "We're not skilled or experienced in Agile."

o Agile is a mentality, a series of values and principles that guide developers and the Product Owner. Work with the values and principles in mind, and that's the best anyone can do.

- "The Product Owner/Scrum Master isn't available enough."

o These core people need to attend daily meetings and periodical meetings but must also make themselves available at other times. This is a problem that requires immediate correction.

The responses listed under these common complaints are what generally applies; however, your team may have unique situations that require a different response. Additionally, Agile Teams can include complaints beyond these issues. Interpersonal problems happen on Agile Teams as well.

The most important element of addressing complaints on an Agile Team is to provide a response or a resolution that promotes trust and relationship building.

Anonymous Complaints on an Agile Team

Most companies have an open-door policy that allows employees to file anonymous complaints to managers, human resources, or key contact people. Anonymous complaints on an Agile Team breed animosity and can ultimately lead the team to failure.

It is frustrating for many people involved to hear that there's a complaint, and that person is not having the courage or the trust with their team to address it directly. If you are the Scrum Master or Product Owner and someone approaches you with an anonymous complaint you might issue these three options for resolution:

1. Arrange for a small meeting with the Scrum Master and two person's involvement in the complaint.

2. Arrange for a group meeting.

3. Opt not to voice the complaint.

Neither the Scrum Master nor the Product Owner is required to address every complaint that comes across their desk. Ultimately, if the person voicing the complaint can't address it openly, then there may be underlying problems of distrust and a lack of communication within the team. If there are issues regarding distrust and communication, then the anonymous complaint is likely secondary to those issues.

Employ Creative Problem Solving – An Agile Developers Best Skill

We've already mentioned that creative problem solving and creative thinking are two skills often sought after in Agile Developers and Scrum Masters. It is these two skills that can resolve most conflict within an Agile Team. However, it may fall on to the Scrum Master or Product Owner to urge the team to use these skills in a different way. Developers will often use creative thinking to their advantage when working on code, looking for elements of a project that could become automated, and building more efficiency into their daily work. Most developers don't rely on creative problem solving or creative thinking when it comes to interpersonal problems and team conflict.

Walk your team through the four steps of creative problem-solving and apply each of these steps to the conflict at hand. Clarify -- Get to the root of the problem. If it is an interpersonal problem,

Then you may need to assess the elements of each person's personality that are leading to conflict. For example, if one team member frequently delivers work later than the team expected it, then the problem could be time management. That individual team member may not realize how long an individual task is going to take them.

However, the team's perception may be that this person is slacking off or making overly ambitious promises. Often the clarification process will be like ripping off a band-aid, the individuals involved may need to be made aware that their perception may be the actual cause of the conflict.

Ideate -- Brainstorm and explore how to resolve this conflict. Now working on an Agile team, there are certain "solutions" that are not available. For example, again, with interpersonal problems, it's not reasonable to have one team member sitting in a separate room or further away from the team because it will ultimately deteriorate the value of the final product. Put your team to work to create ideas and explore what options are available.

Develop -- During the ideate process, you may hear frequent groans of, "but that won't work." The development step demands that people avoid cutting down ideas and instead work shopping those ideas to make them implementable.

Implement -- Implementation is often easier said than done. When you're to the implementation step, ensure that you build follow up within your upcoming meetings. That can include your daily standups and your Sprint meetings. Conflict resolution doesn't stop when you identify a way to resolve the issue. Conflict resolution is complete when the issue is no longer a problem.

Coach Instead of Managing, Facilitate Instead of Directing

Agile team management comes down to coaching and facilitating, while most business practices have taught people they need to manage and direct. It's true. There are some management tactics involved in both the Product Owner and Scrum Master positions. However, within Agile Teams, it's very common for a leader to emerge within the Development Team, and the team still not take on a hierarchical structure.

Every member of an Agile Team must be willing to face challenges and conflict together. Coming back to the core of Agile Principles and the values listed within the Agile Manifesto, the team must always put the product in the project in focus. But if the people don't value each other over the processes and a team structure, then the product won't be as high quality as it could have been. Ultimately if there are conflicts and tension within the team, it could lead to project failure.

But an Agile team experiencing conflict it doesn't mean it's on the road to ruin. If anything, conflict is a good sign that the people within the team are working collaboratively. You can take any group of people, and there will always be different perspectives and approaches, so conflict should be expected. As a leader on an Agile Project, you should aim to coach and facilitate the team through any conflict or complaint rather than making decisions for them or issuing orders to resolve the problem.

Chapter 4: How to Manage Sprints and Sprint Events, and the Backlog

There are three key elements to managing an Agile Team when you get past the people element. You need to be able to manage sprints, Scrum events, and backlog. It is likely that other people may take the reins on managing certain pieces of a sprint, Scrum event, and the Product Owner may even delegate control of the backlog. But it is important that every person of the team understand the core purpose of these three facets of an Agile Project.

One of the common complaints about Agile, or the argument against using Agile, is that there are too many meetings. Because of the emphasis that Agile places on communication, these meetings are necessary. Scrum events and sprints demand a high level of communication, so there won't be the meetings where everyone sits around, not addressing the primary issue. Agile meetings are often restricted on time, highly structured, and exist with a clear purpose.

The Daily Meeting

The daily meeting, the daily Scrum, the Kanban meeting, the daily standup, and many other names all reference the same meeting. Many Agile teams will avoid using the terms Scrum and Kanban because they refer to specific Agile Methodologies. But Scrum and Kanban are also common jargon among Agile Teams, so it's not uncommon to hear them used in reference to this daily meeting.

The daily standup term came from Agile Members standing up during the meeting to keep the meeting as short as possible.

The daily meeting exists to report the status of different tasks and the backlog to the Product Owner. The Scrum Master takes the wheel on the daily meeting by discussing what each person in the team has accomplished, where the project is at currently, and the progress of the current sprint. This is not the meeting to talk about conflicts unless a prior conflict has arisen and is impacting the team's progress.

This particular meeting is the forum for each team member holding the other accountable and for the Product Owner to ask questions. The Scrum Master should serve as the communication conduit during this meeting. They should interpret any answers that the Product Owner didn't fully understand, and help the Development Team understand requests or information from the Product Owner. This meeting is the opportunity to plan out the next few hours.

Tools for the Daily Meeting:

• **Kanban/Scrum Board** – This board, although called a Kanban or Scrum board, is often used in Agile Teams even when they're not using the Kanban or Scrum methodologies.

• **The Parking Lot** – All questions or concerns brought up that aren't pertinent to the work currently being worked on get put in the "parking lot." It's the equivalent of "putting a pin" in something.

• **Timer** – It is important that the meeting only lasts for 15 minutes. If the meetings go longer than this, they can devour the entire day.

• **Project Calendar** – Project calendar outlines the current sprint goals to ensure that daily tasks stay in line with the overarching goals.

What is a Sprint?

A sprint is one of the things that will drive an Agile Team forward. Sprints are another term for iteration, which refers to a short stretch of time when the team works on specific goals. The sprints are typically the heart of the Agile Methodologies, and they help people work within an Agile Team with a minimal amount of frustration. The series of iterations help to bring down giant projects into manageable segments.

Every sprint starts with a sprint planning event. The idea of sprinting is that through careful planning, the team can be in constant motion without being overworked. Sprint planning is done as part of a collaboration between the Product Owner, the Scrum Master, and the Development Team. It involves the entire Agile Team.

Sprint Planning Event

There aren't necessarily hard rules about the sprint planning event, but there are some commonly adopted practices. For example, most Agile teams put a two-hour limit on the sprint planning event. That limit ensures that the meeting only involves sprint planning, and it creates a sense of urgency because two hours might not be enough time to plan out everything. The time limit is a way to keep everyone focused and eliminate unnecessary conversation. Additionally, sprints are usually limited to two-week timeframes.

So why does it take about two hours to map out the next two weeks of work? Initially, the meeting will be led by the Development Team that will assess all of the work needed to deliver on the sprint goal. Typically sprint goals will cover a singular function or achieve a desired effect within the software. The Development Team will initially take the helm and map out what they can or cannot deliver over the next two weeks to achieve this sprint's goal.

Typically the initial sprint might just be planning out the project itself and defining key features or functions expected of the software and the creation of the backlog. That sprint backlog will continue to receive updates or changes after every sprint planning event.

Now, each person should thoroughly prepare for a spring planning event. The Product Owner must ensure that they arrive with an up-to-date backlog, notes from the last sprint review, feedback from the stakeholders, and their vision of the product. The Development Team, if they know of the upcoming sprint, should have not only ideas as to what their task list will look like, but feedback on how the recently finished sprint will impact the next two weeks. Finally, the Scrum Master must come with the updates from the team that the Product Owner needs to hear an in-depth explanation of how those updates will impact this particular sprint planning Event.

You may have begun to notice that with the sprint system, the only thing the team focuses on is the current step or sprint. It's true. Many Agile teams work with a very limited scope of focus for their sprints. However, during these sprint planning events, the team has the opportunity to assess the future of the project. During sprint Review Meetings, they have the opportunity to reflect on future progress, challenges, and setbacks. The Product Owner is the one person who must have a clear line of focus and a big-picture view of the project. All others involved will dedicate their focus to the sprint, and that starts with the sprint planning event and ends with the sprint Retrospective event.

Sprint Review Meetings

Depending on who you speak with, the Sprint Review Meeting is either the most or least important of the sprint meetings. Unlike the sprint planning event or the sprint retrospective, the sprint review is not a formal event.

That doesn't mean that the sprint review is optional. In fact, it is recommended for every team using any methodology of Agile that calls for working in iterations, which is nearly all of them. There is a purpose in keeping them informal in that the team shouldn't "waste" time preparing for a meeting that is really more like a check-up. Some "rules" that exist for sprint review meetings include:

• No PowerPoints
• No more than a certain time spent in the meeting, usually one hour.
• No meeting minutes

What should happen during a sprint review is :

• Review the progress in the sprint
• Discuss the work and demonstrate, if possible
• Identify pain points
• Update status of the sprint
• Collaborate for the remainder of the sprint

The sprint review is the opportunity for the team to come together and assess where they are in the sprint. They may acknowledge each other's accomplishments and demo new features. Additionally, it's one of the times that the team is not so sequestered from everyone else. Participants in these meetings can include the Product Owner, Crum Master, managers, interested businesspersons, and even developers from other projects.

The one thing that should happen during this meeting is that the backlog should receive an update. The Product Owner can do this quietly throughout the meeting and, in the end, review it with the Development Team to ensure that they captured everything. Additionally, the Product Owner's role in this meeting is to assess the quality of the work and bridge any communication gaps when it comes to how a function or feature developed during that sprint should operate.

Sprint Retrospectives

One of the elements that keep Agile Teams together and working collaboratively is the regularly scheduled retrospectives. Sprint retrospectives are the opportunity to focus on continuous improvement, identify the good, and identify the bad. Sprint retrospectives are important, but many in the Agile community feel that these are the most painful areas for the team. Sprinting retrospectives can quickly turn into meetings where one person is getting called out, or people experience a multitude of their ideas being put down.

At a sprint retrospective, the Scrum Master, Product Owner, and Development Team should all be present. This may also be a time where you see executives or higher-level management checking in on the project. However, a sprint retrospective should never focus on the Product Owner, the Scrum Master, or any visitors coming to the meeting. In fact, these meetings should exist exclusively for the Development Team to express themselves. Typically sprint retrospectives are not the platform to introduce change requests or give negative feedback.

The ideal result of a sprint retrospective is that the team will walk away with greater confidence in their self-organized work structure, enable better collaboration, and result in happier developers. Usually, happy developers mean happy end-users. So what needs to happen for a successful sprint retrospective meeting? First, someone must take the reins and set the stage. This usually falls to the Scrum

Master; however, the Product Owner may see this as an opportunity to devote more time to the team. Set a time for everyone to arrive and ensure that the environment is ready before the meeting starts. 2nd, gather the data. Every sprint retrospective meeting must have the most completed and up-to-date version of the backlog and any information pertinent to this particular sprint.

That means that whoever is leading the sprint retrospective meeting should check in with the individual team members to determine if they have data or information that needs to be shared with the team.

The remaining three steps for a successful sprint retrospective meeting will come during the meeting itself. Preparation is important, but the meeting has a purpose, and it's largely to generate insight, make decisions, and close the sprint.

Generating insight will stem from a series of questions that you'll need to ask your team. Common questions include:

- What went well?

- Was there additional motivation during this sprint?

- Did any training, skill, or particular knowledge contribute to the sprint?

- Did anything go wrong?

- Was there anything that posed a particular or unexpected challenge?

- How did the team respond to the challenge?

- If something went wrong, was it because of incorrect implementation, confusion during communication, or an unexpected technology challenge?

- What were the team's learning points?

- Was there information learned during this sprint that could be useful to other teams?

- What actions were implemented and improved work?

• Identify one thing you would have changed during this sprint, and how would you have changed it?

• What strategies worked during this sprint?

If you notice, the flow of these questions goes from positive, to negative, to analysis, two corrective opportunities. This flow leads the negativity a very small window to take hold, but it is that window of assessing what went wrong and how the sprint didn't go as planned that can turn a sprint retrospective from a very productive meeting to a very challenging meeting.

If a Product Owner or Scrum Master is leading this meeting, it may be important for them to realize that they don't have hierarchical power over the team. It is not their duty to course-correct the team or to scold them for things that went wrong during the sprint. They may offer insight into corrective action for the upcoming sprint, or even information that may not have been available to the team. But it is very important that these meetings are discussions that largely revolve around the Development Team, what they think, and their lessons learned.

Do's and Don'ts of Sprint Events

As with most things within the Agile Spectrum, there are no clear rules on sprint events. We've mentioned a few guidelines above, such as sprint planning events not lasting more than two hours or keeping your sprint reviews informal. There are some general guidelines that can help new leaders or people new to project management.
Do:

• Make meetings "safe zones" rather than witch hunts.

• Motivate participation by leading with questions

• Replace "Yes, but..." with "Yes, and..." in every situation

• Understand that shy or introverted people don't want to be called out in a meeting but do having meaningful input. Prompt them for response respectfully.

• Plan your meetings, but remember to remain flexible to change.

• Use sprint events to boost team morale. Say no to distractions, but say yes to fun and engaging conversation.
Don't:

• Allow blame. There is no blame in Agile.

• Don't let negative feelings or emotions fester; address them as quickly as possible.

• Invite people into any sprint event or meeting without discussing it with the team first. No one likes a surprise visit from a high-up manager in a meeting when their work is put on display, or when their progress is under review or receiving critique.

• Strike action points or improvement opportunities. Even if those recommended improvements may need to be scheduled down the line, action points and improvements are signs that the Agile Team is focused on the value of the product.

• Don't spread information about the team or the project without giving the Development Team the lead.

• Always follow one meeting format. Mix it up, and if you're out of ideas to rearrange meeting patterns, then ask your fellow teammates.

What is the Backlog?
Although this chapter looks extensively at the sprints and sprint events, these wouldn't be possible without the backlog.

The backlog is the comprehensive list of tasks that are necessary to execute the larger strategic plan properly. The larger strategic plan may, or may not, be a formal document, but the backlog is a foundational element of Agile, and it drives every sprint.

Without the backlog, the team has no idea what's in store for the next sprint and can't plan out where to begin on the next feature, bug fix, or infrastructure change. Agile teams certainly don't have a hierarchical structure, but the product backlog is the only authoritative source that directs the team throughout the entire project. The product backlog shows each item necessary to move forward with the project; however, it does not guarantee that this set of tasks will result in a successful product.

During sprint planning events, the team will look at the backlog and review each item to determine if it is necessary, valuable and if it is automatable. Additionally, during sprint reviews, the team will use the backlog to determine their progress and identify if there are further along in the sprint than initially planned or if they have fallen behind. During sprint retrospective meetings, the Product Owner will update the backlog, and the team will review the set of items to determine if anything was removed or added for the sake of product value.

Now, backlogs can vary in size, and different Product Owners will involve different levels of detail in the backlog. The core benefit of having a backlog regardless of how detailed or extensive is that it's a placeholder for future tasks and future conversations about the ultimate outcome of this project. The importance of the backlog cannot be understated, and it needs to be an integral part of every sprint event, including daily meetings.

Chapter 5: Keeping the Team and Team Members Accountable

Perhaps the most common question asked when people are new to Agile is, "How are people held accountable?" it is a struggle for many project managers and people on the Development Team because accountability often drives projects. But within Agile projects, each person is responsible for keeping themselves accountable and for keeping the team accountable. Of course, some people naturally need a guiding hand or a little push to get tests done on time or produce the value that's expected of them. How do you help these team members remain accountable to the team and themselves? How, as a Product Owner or a Scrum Master, can you hold yourself accountable to your task and upholding Agile Principles?

When looking at how most business information sources define accountability, there is a pretty clear expectation. Across the board, people refer to accountability as an individual or group upholding their responsibility in terms of performance to a specific function. While this seems very direct many project managers and high-level managers will distort this definition to serve whatever purpose they have at the time. That simply doesn't work in Agile Projects. Agile is so focused on iterations or increments that it is only possible to hold individuals or the team accountable for the current tasks at hand. One of the best ways to do this is to teach accountability so your self-organized team can build autonomy and confidence.

How to Keep a Self-Organized Team Accountable

Traditional management tactics teach us that managers, leaders, and entrepreneurs on any level need to engage employees and push them toward being accountable for their duties. Even when leaders actively avoid micromanagement, they can often get stuck in a parental type of loop where they check in periodically to ensure specific duties have been accomplished. Over time, that can effectively teach people to become self-accountable, and the manager and that employee can build enough trust in moving past those check-ins. But that means that that particular leader has to go through that process with every individual, and if one of those people leaves the team, they have to start over when a replacement comes in. Additionally, Agile Teams don't have the time to teach self-accountability through this time-intensive method.

Build a Culture of Accountability

Many of the Agile Principles help build a culture of accountability. However, there are some elements of accountability that can be muddied or unclear and cause confusion among the Agile Team. This doesn't just apply to Development Team members, but it also applies to the Scrum Master and the Product Owner.

As part of building a culture geared toward accountability, you want to set clear expectations, define individuals' capabilities, and keep clear measurements in place. All of these things you can do during the daily meeting, which means that you're implementing a degree of accountability into the first 15 minutes of everyone's workday. It's an ideal situation that countless other managers wish they could bring onto their teams.

To do this, when you host the daily meeting or when the Product Owner is present for the daily meeting, they should specifically open a window for questions and clarification. Remember that there should be no scoffing or putting down questions because that line of communication is vital to project success. Additionally, the Kanban, or Scrum board, will act as your method of measurement. This visual tool allows the entire team to see who is accomplishing tasks, and who is not.

Have the Much Needed Conversation

Sometimes you just need to sit down and have a one-on-one conversation. Agile teams don't work for everyone, and the unconventional structure can make people realize they have a serious challenge when implementing self-accountability. Self-accountability does not come naturally to most humans. We largely work on external accountability, which is why the hierarchical structure of management serves well in most industries.

If it seems within the first few weeks that someone is standing out as unaccountable or lazy, you may need to sit down and have a chat. This conversation can be hard. However, approaching it from the stance of wanting to gain understanding can make the conversation easier for both you and the team member. Ask them how dedicated they are to the project and how they feel about the current processes and task load they have.

Remember that when you have problems with accountability, it may be caused by the team member feeling overwhelmed. They may be in a state of paralysis where they can't start on one task because there are so many ahead of them. Additionally, they may have never worked in a situation where they're self-accountable. They may need guidance or a set of tools to help them learn how to manage their time.

And be sure that, when you have conversations about accountability, that it's geared toward a productive, or problem solving, result. You don't want to sit down a team member and tell them that they're not doing enough or that they are not meaningful to the team because they are unaccountable.

Don't Let Poor Performance Fester

Poor performance usually isn't something that will show up at the end of a project. Typically poor performers are identifiable within the first week or two of working as a team. Don't allow poor performance to fester. Address it right away either in a one-on-one meeting or with the Scrum Master involved.

When addressing poor performance, it's important to cite specific instances and refrain from using definitive statements. For example, you don't want to say, "Johnny, you never bring anything into the daily meeting." This statement does not cite a specific example, and there are likely times that Johnny had brought something into the meeting. Instead, you might phrase it like this, "Johnny over the last week during the daily meetings you haven't had any updates on your tasks where are you at in terms of progress?"

Consider the Rest of the Team

If you've done all of the above and still have trouble with one or two team members, it's time to take it a step further. It may be easy to confront an employee or team member who is clearly letting down the rest of the team.

But, once you're sitting down and having that discussion or you're able to hear their side of the story, it can become very difficult. We mentioned earlier having the much-needed conversation of getting to the root of the problem period, but there are times when people don't respond to internal or external accountability, and it can lead a project to failure.

If you're struggling with confronting an employee who simply doesn't seem to understand accountability, consider the feelings of the rest of the team. How is Brittney supposed to feel when Jenny never completed her tasks for a sprint? How should Sean feel when Gerald suspiciously misses days when meetings are scheduled? If you're finding it difficult to implement accountability practices, consider the remainder of the team; the people who are working hard.

Helping Teams Adjust to Agile Accountability and Management Tactics

A running joke among developers is that Agile Accountability is an oxymoron. To some degree, it's true. On a typical project, the team will have one clear manager, and that manager may report to a project director or coordinator. That clear line of communication ensures that one person is ultimately in charge of all the decision-making, and everyone else is working to execute their plan.

On an Agile team, that's not the case. But many of your Agile Team members may have already become accustomed to simply being told what to do and then following orders.

You will need to help your team adjust to Agile Accountability and to move away from traditional management tactics. This may be as hard for you as it is for them.

One of the best ways to approach this transition is to guide accountability with questions. If someone asks you, "What is the deadline for this?" You can respond with, "How much time do you need to complete it?" when you put the emphasis on their abilities you give them the opportunity to set a reasonable deadline for themselves, set an early deadline that may lead to a lower value, or set a late deadline which may lead to lower productivity. Often the initial answers won't be extremely accurate, but after the first few weeks, your team should start to understand how long certain tasks do take and then provide a more accurate scope of time.

But of course, time isn't the only issue when it comes to accountability. For example, someone on your team may lack the skillset or knowledge to complete one of the tasks during a particular Sprint. They may at first be hesitant to expose that they don't have the know-how, but part of accountability is owning up to knowledge gaps. Again, going back to the earlier definition, you're responsible for completing a certain function or duty, and that means seeking out the knowledge or closing that knowledge gap to fulfill that responsibility. You can address this issue by creating a culture of ongoing learning or continuous improvement.

There are many aspects of working on an Agile Team that are far different from working on a typical project.

The challenges your team faces in adjustment will vary dependent on the people involved. It's up to you as either the Scrum Master or Product Owner to identify where you need to help your team adjust and what management tactics can stay and which need to go.

Increments and Updates

The method of working in iterations or increments allows one of the best ways to teach accountability to arise naturally. Public praise and positivity within a team not only improves team morale, but it helps heighten the accountability of every single team member. Not everyone on the team has to be Mr. Positivity, but it certainly helps when everyone on the team gets some sort of recognition when they meet a goal or complete a task.

The daily meeting updates and Sprint review meetings are specific times dedicated to acknowledging the people who have accomplished something on their task list or stricken something off the backlog.

Use the Agile structure of increments and updates to help build this type of public praise and replace consequences with rewards. Additionally, increments and updates allow Product Owners and Scrum Masters to develop accountability the same way that athletic coaches do. Coaches pushed their athletes to practice with an intense focus even though it's not a game. They use drills, scrimmages, and practice runs to continue improvement and continue learning.

That effort of constantly getting better and constantly working with a hyper-focus also helps to build accountability. You'll see as you move from iteration to iteration, or from Sprint to Sprint, that your team members will naturally continue to build their accountability skills.

Collective Skill Sets

There is one action that anyone on an Agile Team can take to improve accountability for the entire day of the project greatly. Most teams get held back from a responsible state because they are stuck in a problem-identifying mode rather than engaging their creative problem solving and pooling their skill sets together. It happens the same way that a virus spreads. One person feels that they don't understand the problem, but the work is their responsibility, so they're going to move forward with what they have available.

What they don't consider is that one of the resources available is the collective knowledge of the team. So what happens when the next person doesn't understand something or stumbles across a knowledge gap is they also don't ask her question, because no one else has. This continues until the entire team is working in silos, and they're unable to come together in a meaningful way to deliver a valuable product.

One of the big factors that come into play here is interdependence. As a whole, our society highly values the ability to work and function independently.

Because of that, many people are rightfully shy about exposing areas that they're unfamiliar with or asking for help. This ties directly into accountability because, often, people will drag out tasks trying to learn something on their own rather than going back to that original Agile principle of collaborating with their team. Again accountability refers to not just the individual but the group. At some point, you have to move beyond keeping individual team members accountable, and keeping the group accountable so that tasks can remain on track.

To start building accountability for the entire team, you'll need to encapsulate them with their commitments to the project. Take the private moments of hesitancy and embarrassment regarding skill gaps out of the picture. Collaborate in public as a team and encourage people to be honest about what they don't know so that the skill sets can be shared and collective. Assure team members that even the least experienced person on the team likely has a skill or knowledge that other members on the team don't have.

Keep in mind that accountability, responsibility, and trust are closely intertwined. Sometimes it may seem harsh to aggressively pursue a new value system and push people to become interdependent. But in Agile team cannot work with a collection of five independent individual developers working separately on the same project. Agile projects demand collaboration, and when collaboration doesn't exist within an Agile Team, the result is product failure.

How to Direct Teams Toward Collective Skill Sets

To put a focus on building collective skill sets, you may encourage the team to not only help one another when each other needs it but to host mini-lessons or mini-meetings. Some Scrum Masters or Product Owners encouraged the team to do this in the five or 10 minutes after the daily meeting. Team members can take turns rotating and use those five or 10 minutes to share a skill that they believe would benefit the rest of the team. Even if this is a skill that other team members are already familiar with or a bit of knowledge that is not necessarily new, it can spark discussion about the use of the knowledge or skill and different perspectives on what this information means to the team.

Additionally, you may encourage the team to build a knowledge database, adding information as they go through iterations. Or, issue a checklist and have people mark what skills they have or what segments of development knowledge their most comfortable handling. A database or a list to reference can help people identify exactly who they should talk to when they have a question. It can save your Development Team time from asking each individual if they can help with something on a task. Instead, they can reference the list or database and identify that John or Brittany is most familiar with that particular skill.

A final suggestion is to use one of the tools you're already employing as part of your Agile Project for a collective skill platform. For example, in Trello, or Monday, where you can have a digital Kanban board, you may have a particular list with a set of cards for skills and knowledge sharing.

While you may have an additional list for problem sharing, that way, if one of your team members runs into a challenge where they may need to pull on the help or knowledge of others within the team, they can add a card on to that list stating their problem. When the teammates check the list and see the card, someone with that knowledge set can pick it up and message the person or go over to their desk to help them.

Chapter 6: Tools to Assist Scrum Masters and Project Leaders

Although it's always important to remember that al jail will always value people in interactions over tools and processes, it never hurts to have a good tool available to your team. Of course, not all tools are made equal, and some tools will fall just shy of meeting your team's needs while others will offer so many features they become complicated and less useful. Here are a small handful of tools that can help Scrum Masters and Product Owners keep the team focused, and keep the project on track.

Tools for Integration and Source Control

As part of the Agile Principles, automation is very important to a Development Team. If something can be automated, it should be automated. Use these two tools to help automate some of your Development Teams' most tedious tasks.

Git

Git is a source control tool. It serves the purpose of giving the team more flexibility. I'm allowing developers to merge their code at a later time. It helps teams keep their code organized, and can even help keep track of different versions.

Jenkins

Jenkins is a continuous integration tool similar to Git, but there are a few core differences. Jenkins serves more as an automation server. It allows teams to build and test software projects while integrating changes as the team makes progress. It is open source and has a host of plugins.

Team Tools for Project Management

Although Agile, either breaks or outright ignore a lot of the rules of standard project management, you're still working on a project. The people involved in the team and in providing the resources necessary to finish the project need to have a clear line of sight on where tasks are currently at and what's coming next.

Monday

Monday really supports the project management elements of Agile Teams. It provides reporting, time tracking, planning tools, and a calendar, which can be very useful. Monday also gives the team the opportunity to choose between working in a Kanban system, in charts as in a dashboard, or with a timeline similar to a traditional project management approach.

Monday also integrates with a variety of third-party applications, which can make it really desirable for the Product Owner and businesspersons involved in the project. One of the troubles that teams can face with Monday is that it has so many features it's easy to overcomplicate this tool. This is one of those instances where you may have to weigh the benefit of the tool against the needs of the people on your team.

Trello

Trello has been praised as a secret weapon or powerhouse tool for Agile work. It has withstood any criticism that has come its way and supports almost every element of the Agile manifesto. Trello is easy to use, simple and aligns exactly with the Scrum framework. People can create numerous boards that are either personal or teamwork spaces.

Those boards contain lists, and on those lists are cards that stand as tasks—all the cards you can insert checklists, tags, files, and add comments.

Essentially people love Trello because it works exactly like a Kanban or Scrum board but in digital form.

Old-School Kanban Board

You'll be hard-pressed to find an Agile Team that doesn't use an old school Kanban or Scrum board. These boards are usually a whiteboard or a wall with columns that show the progress and tasks within the current Sprint. They use cards, and the card will move from one column to the next depending on who's working on it, if that task requires additional resources, and if that task is stuck in one way or another.

Both of the tools above, Monday and Trello, aimed to recreate the old school Kanban or Scrum board. However, given how much technology has integrated into our daily work lives, many developers feel more comfortable having a digital version of this board, in addition to a physical version that they can see every day.

Tools for Collaborating and Communicating

With communication and collaboration being so important to Agile, it's no wonder that many companies have tried to make tools just for helping Agile Teams communicate. There is some need for precaution with these tools, because as they become more complex, it may make it more difficult for your team to communicate.

Slack

Slack allows teams to communicate by allowing people on the project to create Discussion boards and channels. Then within those channels and discussions, every member can alert or call attention to a message from other members and add tags.

This is exceptionally helpful for ensuring that a message gets to the right person. This can also be helpful for connecting teams that may be working remotely or distantly from each other. But the many changes in Standard work methods for software developer's tools like this can allow people to work remotely and still work collaboratively.

One element that does make slacks stand out from very similar software options is that it integrates with other tools built specifically for Agile Teams such as Trello and intercom. It does come with many advanced features, but when using slack on a basic level, it's easy to maintain those core principles around simplicity.

Asana

Asana is a communication tool disguised as a project management tool. Although at first, it seems that it's only for organizing large projects, Asana really excels in helping people communicate on specific tasks across a single large project.

Asana allows members to tag others in messages and in tasks as well as assigning due dates or scheduling tasks to each other. The downside of Asana is exactly what makes it desirable. Its wide array of project management tools, such as being able to assign tasks and monitor deadlines, generally goes against Agile Principles.

This is one of those tools that might be great for the Development Team but could be something that the Product Owner might not have a role in, especially if there's a chance that the Product Owner could overstep their duties and start taking more of a hierarchical role in the team.

Determining Which Tools to Use

It can be a challenge deciding which tools are right to use for your team, especially when you're supposed to be emphasizing the importance of people over the function of tools. The tools available to Agile Teams have changed drastically since the Agile Manifesto was written in 2001. Additionally, many of these tools, such as Trello and Monday, were created expressly for Agile Teams.

If you want to bring in more tools but aren't sure where to start, discuss it with your team. It's possible that the developers on your team are familiar with some of these tools. They may have had experiences that would cause them to encourage or discourage the use of those tools. However, some tools such as Git or Jenkins may be suggested by your Development Team in an effort to automate as much as possible.

When determining the tools that are right for your team and for your project, always remember to employ the creative problem skillset within your team. It may be that none of these tools serve your needs but that there are others available, or internal systems within your company that can help automate and simplify your project.

Always return to that core philosophy of people over tools. These tools are helpful, and our teams are working in a modern age that largely demands digital integration. However, some tools, such as a Scrum board, work best in their physical form. It may be that many of these technology-driven or digital tools will serve to supplement the team's work rather than direct it.

It may seem as though not using any tools would be most aligned with agile principles, but that's not usually conducive to a large project. When you are helping to guide both the team and the project, tools can simplify complex procedures and make some goals more attainable. Of course, you may always need to fall back onto the more traditional tools or systems mentioned throughout this book, such as the backlog, sprint events, and one-on-one meetings. Agile also has multiple methodologies that may call for different structures or an even more unconventional approach to a project.

Conclusion

Ultimately, Agile Principles should guide you and your team through the project. Doing that means understanding the Agile Manifesto, the core values, and how the principles should apply within your team. Your team should guide the project, and managers should look to the Development Team for direction. It is a very hands-off or removed approach to management and can be hard to adopt at first. But after getting involved with the developers and seeing the power of a self-organized team, it's easy to continue adopting Agile Methods.

By now, you should have learned all the tools that you need to implement accountability and collaboration within your Agile Team. Use your experiences from working with people and leading teams to help bridge communication and help resolve conflicts. It is important that you and your team are put first. Perhaps the most vital element of Agile is that the people always remain more important than the tools, and the value of the product remains more important than the processes. If you keep these in mind and listen to your team, you should have a successful Agile Project.

Resources

http://www.Agilenutshell.com

https://techbeacon.com/app-dev-testing/agility-beyond-history-legacy-Agile-development

https://www.wrike.com/project-management-guide/faq/what-Agile-is-not/

https://kanbanize.com/blog/right-Agile-methodology-for-your-project/

https://www.infoq.com/articles/Agile-goal-setting-appelo/

https://www.blueprintsys.com/Agile-development-101/Agile-methodologies

https://AgileManifesto.org

https://www.playbookhq.co/blog/Agile-principle-1

https://platinumedge.com/blog/supporting-Agile-principle-2-welcome-changes

http://marcbless.blogspot.com/2011/03/Agile-principle-3-frequent-delivery.html

https://platinumedge.com/blog/supporting-Agile-principle-4-business-developer-partnerships-through-collocated-teams

https://technology.amis.nl/2008/03/02/Agile-software-development-the-principles-principle-5-build-projects-around-motivated-individuals/

https://www.frontrowAgile.com/blog/posts/23-the-problem-with-the-6th-Agile-principle-on-communication

https://platinumedge.com/blog/supporting-Agile-principle-7-working-products

https://www.pmguaranteed.com/what-is-Agile-sustainable-pace/

https://technology.amis.nl/2008/12/28/Agile-software-development-the-principles-principle-9-continuous-attention-to-technical-excellence-and-good-design-enhances-agility/

https://computerhistory.org/profile/linus-torvalds/

https://quotefancy.com/quote/1445832/Linus-Torvalds-Avoiding-complexity-reduces-bugs

https://www.productplan.com/glossary/Agile-principles/

https://www.compuware.com/Scrum-teams-whats-Scrum-meetings/

https://www.Scrum.org/resources/what-is-a-product-owner
Scrum Master definition

https://redbooth.com/blog/main-roles-Agile-team

https://www.wrike.com/project-management-guide/Agile-project-management-tools-techniques/

https://www.Agileconnection.com/article/handling-conflict-Agile-teams-what-do-when-team-member-complains

https://www.mindtools.com/pages/article/creative-problem-solving.htm

https://www.Agiledad.com/post/2018/05/08/daily-standup-increasing-team-accountability

https://www.Scrum.org/resources/blog/accountability-quality-Agile

https://www.mindtools.com/CommSkll/RunningMeetings.htm

https://www.atlassian.com/Agile/Scrum/sprints

https://www.atlassian.com/Agile/Scrum/sprint-planning

https://www.mountaingoatsoftware.com/Agile/Scrum/meetings/sprint-review-meeting

https://backlog.com/blog/successful-sprint-review-meeting/

https://www.visual-paradigm.com/Scrum/what-is-sprint-retrospective-meeting/

https://softwaredevtools.com/blog/dos-donts-Agile-retrospectives/

https://blog.aspiresys.pl/case-studies/7-dos-donts-sprint-retrospective/

https://www.investopedia.com/terms/a/accountability.asp

https://hbr.org/2016/01/the-right-way-to-hold-people-accountable

https://www.insperity.com/blog/improve-accountability-workplace-5-steps/

https://www.Agilealliance.org/is-Agile-accountability-an-oxymoron/

https://learn.truesport.org/teach-accountability-positive/

https://www.leadingAgile.com/2014/12/time-accountability-Agile-teams/
https://blog.arkadin.com/en/collective-knowledge-four-reasons-your-company-must-become-collaborative/
https://git-scm.com
https://www.jenkins.io
https://www.edureka.co/blog/what-is-jenkins/
https://monday.com/s/Agile-management-software
https://blog.hubstaff.com/Agile-trello/
https://resources.workable.com/tutorial/collaboration-tools

Printed in Great Britain
by Amazon

83952986R00048